ZIONSVILLE PUBLIC LIBRARY

W9-BZY-172

ZPL

**DIFFICULT &
DANGEROUS**

Mountain Adventures

ALEX BROWN

A⁺

Smart Apple Media

Hussey-Mayfield Memorial
Public Library
Zionsville, IN 46077

Smart Apple Media is published by Black Rabbit Books
P.O. Box 3263, Mankato, Minnesota 56002

U.S. publication copyright © 2009 Black Rabbit Books. International copyright reserved in all countries. No part of this book may be reproduced in any form without written permission from the publisher.

Printed in Hong Kong

Library of Congress Cataloging-in-Publication Data

Brown, Alex, 1975–
    Mountain adventures / Alex Brown.
    p. cm.—(Smart Apple Media. Difficult & dangerous)
    Includes index.
    Summary: "The true stories of Edward Whymper, Edmund Hillary and Tenzing Norgay, the Andes plane crash survivors, Arlene Blum, and Joe Simpson and Simon Yates, who survived harrowing experiences in the mountains"-Provided by publisher.
    ISBN 978-1-59920-157-3
    1. Mountaineering accidents—Juvenile literature. 2. Wilderness survival—Juvenile literature. I. Title.
GV200.B76 2009
796.522—dc22

                                                                                    2008000433

Created by Q2AMedia
Series Editor: Jean Coppendale
Book Editor: Paul Manning
Senior Art Designers: Ashita Murgai, Nishant Mudgal
Designer: Shilpi Sarkar
Picture Researcher: Lalit Dalal
Line Artists: Amit Tayal, Sibi N.D
Illustrators: Mahender Kumar, Sanyogita Lal

All words in **bold** can be found in the glossary on pages 30–31.

Web site information is correct at time of going to press. However, the publishers cannot accept liability for any information or links found on third-party Web sites.

Picture credits
t=top b=bottom c=center l=left r=right m=middle
Cover: Q2AMedia
Stock Connection/ Alamy: 4, Arlene Blum: 5, Getty Images: 6t, Alpine Club: 6b,
Peter Wey/ Shutterstock: 7, Mary Evans Picture Library/ Photolibrary: 8, 9,
Stapleton Collection/ Corbis: 10, Bruce Yeung/ Shutterstock: 11, Alfred Gregory/
Royal Geographical Society: 13, Edmund Hillary/ Royal Geographical Society: 14,
Associated Press: 15, Group of Survivors/ Corbis: 18, 19, 20, Arlene Blum: 21, 22,
Pichugin Dmitry/ Shutterstock: 23, Cheryl: 26, Touching the Void/ Rex Features: 27, 29

9 8 7 6 5 4 3 2 1

Contents

HIGH ADVENTURE   4

MAN AGAINST MOUNTAIN   6
Edward Whymper and the Ascent of the Matterhorn

ON TOP OF THE WORLD   11
The Story of the 1953 British Everest Expedition

ALIVE AGAINST THE ODDS   16
The Story of the Andes Plane Crash Survivors

ASSAULT ON ANNAPURNA 1   21
*Arlene Blum and the First All–Woman Expedition
to the Himalayas*

TO HELL AND BACK   26
The Incredible Story of Joe Simpson and Simon Yates

Glossary   30

Index and Web Finder   32

HIGH ADVENTURE

From the earliest times, climbers have risked their lives in attempts to climb the world's highest mountains. They have faced freezing temperatures, rock falls, and great personal danger. Even though many peaks have now been conquered, the challenge of mountaineering is as powerful as ever.

A climber uses his ice ax to scale a wall of snow and ice high in the French Alps.

First to Climb Everest?

In 1924, the young British climber and explorer George Mallory set out to become the first man to climb the world's highest mountain. Mallory already knew how dangerous Everest could be. Three years earlier, he had narrowly escaped death when an **avalanche** swept down on his party, killing all seven of his **Sherpa** porters.

On June 8, Mallory and his climbing partner, Andrew Irvine, were spotted high up on the North **Ridge**, just a few hundred yards from the summit. It was the last time they were seen alive. Mallory's fate remained a mystery until 1999, when his body was found by climbers, perfectly preserved in the ice. Did Mallory reach the summit that day in 1924? We will probably never know.

Testing Endurance

Since Mallory's time, many of the highest mountains in the world have been conquered. But climbers are still finding plenty of new ways to test their skills and stamina.

In the 1970s, the Italian climber Reinhold Messner completed a spectacular series of Alpine rock climbs without the use of **metal pegs**. In 1978, he teamed up with Peter Habeler to achieve the incredible feat of climbing Everest without oxygen (see below). Still not satisfied, Messner repeated the feat in 1980—this time, climbing solo!

The amazing stories in this book prove that as long as mountains exist, there will be challenges to be met and exciting mountain adventures to be had.

"Breathing becomes such a serious business we scarcely have strength to go on . . . I no longer belong to myself and to my eyesight. I am nothing more than a single narrow gasping lung, floating over the mists and summits."

From Reinhold Messner, *Everest: Expedition to the Ultimate* (1979)

Hazards of Mountaineering

To survive at high altitude, most climbers need to wear breathing apparatus and carry supplies of bottled oxygen.

Mountain ranges, such as the Alps, Himalayas, and Andes, are among the most dangerous natural environments on the planet. Freezing temperatures, **blizzards**, rock falls, and avalanches are obvious hazards. But just as deadly is the effect of altitude.

At heights of more than 26,250 feet (8,000 m), a lack of oxygen causes many basic body functions to shut down. Every movement takes superhuman effort. In the thin mountain air, many climbers collapse with exhaustion and never wake up again.

MAN AGAINST MOUNTAIN
Edward Whymper and the Ascent of the Matterhorn

In July 1865, an unknown English climber became one of the most talked-about men of the Victorian Age. Edward Whymper was the first man to climb the legendary Swiss mountain, the Matterhorn. But he earned his glory at a terrible cost.

Whymper first became obsessed with climbing during a visit to the Alps in the early 1860s, when a team of climbers invited him to join them on an expedition. Climbing then was very different from today, and equipment was basic (see below). But Whymper was so excited by the experience that he was soon setting off on mountain adventures of his own.

Edward Whymper (1840–1911) was a key figure in the "Golden Age of Alpinism." During this period (1850–65), many of the highest mountains in the Alps were climbed for the first time.

Mountaineering Then and Now

Edward Whymper would have used a tent like this on his early climbing expeditions in the Alps.

Today, climbers carry everything from lightweight tents to **satellite navigation** equipment. But in the early days, pioneers often set out for the summit with little more than a jacket, a hat, a stick or ice ax, and a pair of leather boots.

Equipment was crude and often unreliable. Tents (left) were made of heavy canvas and gave little protection against the cold. Accidents were frequent. Many climbers plunged to their deaths when ropes snapped or metal climbing pegs failed.

The Matterhorn

By the mid-1860s, Whymper had scaled nearly all the highest mountains in the Alps. But he knew that the ultimate test was still ahead of him.

Whymper had already attempted to climb the Matterhorn from the Italian side and had been forced back by the steep rock. But in 1865, he decided to take a route that had never been tried before. He was spurred on by rumors that Italian climbers were planning a rival expedition. Determined not to be beaten to the **summit**, Whymper prepared for the climb of his life.

Towering over the ski resort of Zermatt on the Swiss–Italian border, the Matterhorn is one of the most feared of all Alpine mountains. Each of its four faces is steep, icy, and treacherous. Frequent avalanches send huge falls of ice, rock, and snow crashing down onto the glaciers below.

Map showing the location of the Matterhorn on the Swiss–Italian border

Triumph and Tragedy

Whymper's decision to climb the Matterhorn from the eastern side paid off. On July 14, a party consisting of Whymper, Charles Hudson, Lord Francis Douglas, Douglas Hadow, Michel Croz, and two Peter Taugwalders (father and son) successfully scaled the mountain and found themselves standing in triumph on the summit. They were even more pleased to see the Italian team far below, still struggling up the Italian Ridge.

Whymper and his team were ecstatic. They could not wait to tell the world what they had achieved. None of them knew that a terrible tragedy was about to strike.

"The higher we rose, the more intense became the excitement. What if we should be beaten at the last moment? . . . At 1:40 P.M. the world was at our feet, and the Matterhorn was conquered. Hurrah! Not a footstep could be seen."

From Edward Whymper, *Scrambles Among the Alps* (1871)

This picture shows the excitement of the climbers as they were the first to scale the summit of the Matterhorn.

Death Plunge

The seven climbers cautiously began their descent, linked together by rope. Hadow slipped, knocking Croz off his feet and dragging Hudson and Douglas with him. To the horror of the remaining three men, the thin rope connecting them to the other members of the party broke and the four climbers plunged to their deaths on the Matterhorn Glacier 4,600 feet (1,400 m) below.

Paralyzed

Stunned, the three survivors clung to the steep rock. "For the space of half an hour," Whymper wrote later, "we remained on the spot without moving a single step. The two Taugwalders, paralyzed by terror, cried like infants and trembled in such a manner as to threaten us with the fate of the others."

After a nightmarish descent, the shaken survivors finally reached Zermatt the following morning. A quickly organized search party recovered the broken bodies of Croz, Hadlow, and Hudson. Nothing was found of the fourth man, Lord Francis Douglas, except a shoe, a pair of gloves, and a coat sleeve.

Three days later, on July 17, an Italian party led by Whymper's long-time rival Jean Carrel reached the summit from the Italian side.

Terrors of the Matterhorn

Unstable rock, avalanches, and sudden, violent storms make the Matterhorn one of the most dangerous mountains in the world. As many as 15 climbers die each year attempting to climb the Matterhorn—more than any other Alpine mountain.

"They passed from our sight uninjured, disappeared one by one, and fell from precipice to precipice on to the Matterhorn glacier below . . . From the moment the rope broke it was impossible to help them."

From Edward Whymper, *Scrambles Among the Alps* (1871)

Aftermath of a Tragedy

Whymper's conquest of the Matterhorn brought him fame, but also notoriety. Following the tragedy, many hard questions were asked. Why did Douglas Hadlow lose his footing? Why did the rope break? Why was Whymper not able to produce the rope afterwards to show as evidence?

Whymper went on to climb many other mountains. But he could never forget the tragic death of his four companions. As he grew older, he became more and more solitary and remote. After successful mountaineering expeditions in South America, Greenland, and the Canadian Rockies, Whymper died of natural causes in Switzerland in 1911.

"Climb if you will, but remember that courage and strength are nought without prudence, and that a momentary negligence may destroy the happiness of a lifetime."

From Edward Whymper,
Scrambles Among the Alps (1871)

Spot the Difference

1   Look at the picture on the left. What differences do you think there might be between the equipment shown here and the gear that climbers use today?

2   Could you be a mountaineer? Which of these reasons would make you want to climb a mountain?

   • Breathtaking scenery

   • Danger and excitement

   • Chance to win fame and glory

   • Challenge of testing yourself against extreme conditions

   • Comradeship and team spirit

   • Chance to be the first at something

   What part of climbing would be most likely to put you off?

ON TOP OF THE WORLD

The Story of the 1953 British Everest Expedition

On May 29, 1953, Edmund Hillary of New Zealand and Tenzing Norgay of Nepal achieved one of the greatest feats in the history of mountaineering.

That morning, the two men reached the summit of Everest in the Himalayas (right), becoming the first human beings to stand on the summit of the world's highest mountain.

The achievement of Hillary and Tenzing caught the imagination of the world and made them famous overnight. But how did the two men succeed, when so many other climbers had been defeated by blizzards, freezing temperatures, and raging winds?

Soaring 29,029 feet (8,848 m) above sea level, Everest was created millions of years ago by the powerful forces below Earth's surface that crush and squeeze continents together. The process continues to this day, lifting the entire Himalayan range by a few millimeters each year.

Everest: Triumphs and Disasters

1924	British climbers Mallory and Irvine disappear near summit.
1953	Hillary and Tenzing reach summit.
1963	First Americans reach summit.
1980	Reinhold Messner becomes first to climb Everest solo without oxygen.
1989	First two women, both American, reach the summit.
1996	Eleven climbers die during spring expeditions.

Preparing for the "Death Zone"

Behind Hillary and Tenzing's success was a story of careful planning and organization. The two men were part of a 400-member team including some of the world's best climbers, a physiotherapist, a doctor, a cameraman, a writer from the London newspaper the *Times*, and a small army of Sherpa porters.

The expedition leader, Colonel John Hunt, made sure that the climbers had the best equipment, including specially made high-altitude boots, lightweight tents, shortwave radios, and ladders for bridging crevasses. Oxygen was an essential part of their kit. In the "death zone" above 26,250 feet (8,000 m), survival was possible only for a short period. Without oxygen, climbers risked exhaustion, loss of consciousness, and death.

The Plan

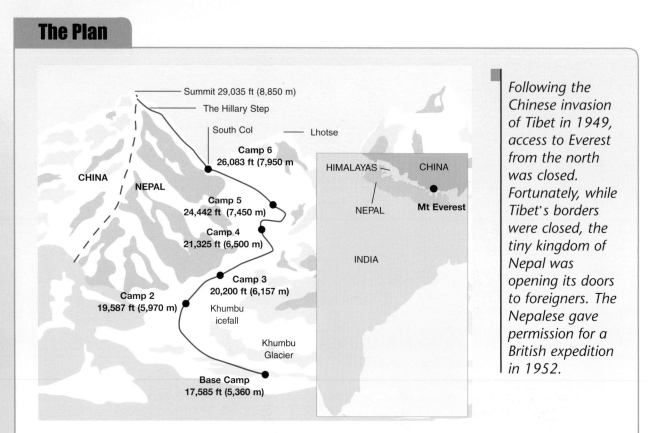

Summit 29,035 ft (8,850 m)
The Hillary Step
South Col — Lhotse
Camp 6 26,083 ft (7,950 m)
CHINA
NEPAL
Camp 5 24,442 ft (7,450 m)
Camp 4 21,325 ft (6,500 m)
Camp 3 20,200 ft (6,157 m)
Camp 2 19,587 ft (5,970 m)
Khumbu icefall
Khumbu Glacier
Base Camp 17,585 ft (5,360 m)

HIMALAYAS — CHINA
NEPAL   Mt Everest
INDIA

Following the Chinese invasion of Tibet in 1949, access to Everest from the north was closed. Fortunately, while Tibet's borders were closed, the tiny kingdom of Nepal was opening its doors to foreigners. The Nepalese gave permission for a British expedition in 1952.

Hunt's plan was to climb Everest from the Nepalese side. Climbers would scale the mountain in stages, setting up camps along the way. Supplies would be carried up the mountain by porters. The expedition took with it 9 tons (8.3 t) of equipment contained in 443 packages, each numbered and listed down to the last matchbox. Their contents included supplies and equipment for a three-month stay.

Hillary and Tenzing, seen here preparing for their final assault on the summit. Lanky and big-boned, Hillary (left) was a beekeeper by profession. The small and wiry Tenzing (right) was a professional Sherpa mountain guide. For both men, climbing Everest was a lifelong dream.

The Khumbu Icefall

On April 12, Hunt and his team set up **base camp** beside the awesome Khumbu Icefall, a frozen **cascade** of jagged ice at the foot of the mountain. A special team began to prepare the way up this treacherous stretch of glacier that was continually moving and groaning under their feet. Camp 2 was pitched halfway up the icefall, but had to be abandoned because of the danger from **crevasses** and gigantic blocks of tumbling ice. Amazingly, the team and the Sherpas managed to carve a route through the Khumbu Icefall without mishap or injury.

"We make ready. We will climb it. This time, with God's help, we will climb on to the end."

From Tenzing Norgay, *Tiger of the Snows* (1955)

13

Assault and Conquest

On May 21, 1953, the first climbing team made it to the South Col (see map, page 12)—a crucial milestone for the expedition. Now Hunt faced a difficult decision. Of the 14 climbers in the party, only 4 would get a chance at the summit. Whom would he choose?

On May 26, the first summit party comprising of Tom Bourdillon and Charles Evans set off. After a promising start, they climbed to a height of 28,750 feet (8,763 m) before bad weather and problems with their oxygen equipment forced them to turn back. Weary and disappointed, they returned to camp.

The Final Bid

The next pair chosen by Hunt were Hillary and Tenzing. On the morning of May 29, the two men woke early and found that Hillary's boots had frozen solid in the night. After thawing them out, the pair were soon trudging their way through the snow. With mounting excitement, they overtook the point reached by Bourdillon and Evans. Then they found their progress blocked by a wall of sheer rock.

His face hidden behind his oxygen mask, Tenzing Norgay stands on the summit of Everest. Flying from his ice ax are the flags of Britain, India, the United Nations, and Nepal.

The "Hillary Step"

After scaling the rock face, later christened the "Hillary Step," the pair were astounded to find themselves standing on an exposed area of snow with nothing but air all around them. It was the summit! With oxygen running low, they could only spend 15 minutes there, taking pictures and hugging each other in sheer delight. As they rejoined the other members of the team, the full realization of what they had achieved began to sink in.

Heroes of Everest

The success of the British Everest Expedition changed mountaineering forever. A hero among his own people, Tenzing Norgay was awarded the George Medal. Hunt and Hillary both received knighthoods. Hillary continued to climb, but devoted much of the rest of his life to the welfare of the Sherpa people, founding schools and hospitals throughout the remote regions of the Himalayas.

> "I continued hacking steps along the ridge and then up a few more to the right . . . to my great delight I realized we were on top of Mount Everest and that the whole world [was] spread out below us."
>
> From Edmund Hillary, *High Adventure* (1955)

Could YOU Survive at High Altitude?

1 Two of the early warning signs of altitude sickness are dizziness and inability to think clearly and make decisions. Why do you think these are especially dangerous for a mountaineer?

2 As Hillary and Tenzing prepared for the assault on the summit of Everest, Hillary feared a "psychological barrier, which might cause us to reach the summit but then collapse."

What do you think he meant?

Hillary and Tenzing were photographed shortly after making their successful summit bid.

ALIVE AGAINST THE ODDS

The Story of the Andes Plane Crash Survivors

On Friday, October 13, 1972, a Uruguayan Air Force plane crashed in the Andes Mountains. The stunned survivors were hopelessly lost in one of the most remote and hostile places on earth. Weakened by starvation, extreme cold, and the stark knowledge that rescue would never come, their ordeal is one of the most harrowing and difficult stories of survival ever told.

On board the plane was a team of young rugby players from Stella Maris College, Montevideo, Uruguay, bound for a match in Santiago, Chile. Despite the bad weather, the players, their relatives, and friends were in high spirits as the plane soared over the snowcapped mountains.

Following the crash, survivors from the Fairchild FH-227D desperately try to attract the attention of a passing rescue plane. In the area where the plane crashed, the mountains rose to 14,760 feet (4,500 m) and were covered with 20 to 100 feet (6 to 30 m) of snow.

But as they headed for Curicó on the western side of the Andes, the weather worsened. The plane began to shake and lurch. As the pilot prepared for an emergency landing over the border between Chile and Argentina, the plane plowed into the side of a mountain. It lost its wings and tail and catapulted down the slope. Of the 45 people on board, 12 died almost instantly. Six more died of their injuries in the days that followed.

Search and Rescue

As soon as **air traffic control** in Santiago lost contact with the Uruguayan plane, a search was organized. But the rescuers had little hope of finding survivors. They knew that the temperature in the mountains dropped at night to 30 or 40 degrees below zero. Any passengers who survived the crash would almost certainly die of cold during their first night on the mountain.

Soon search parties from three countries joined in the hunt for survivors. Rescue planes even passed directly over the scene of the crash, but because the Fairchild FH-227D was white and blended with the snow, it was impossible to spot from the air. Eight days after the search began, it was abandoned.

Map showing the location of the crash and the plane's route from Montevideo in Uruguay to Santiago in Chile

17

Struggle for Survival

Huddled around a small radio that they had found in the wreckage, the survivors listened in shocked silence to the news that the search had been called off. They knew now that they were on their own. What followed was an incredible story of courage and survival.

The students' plight was desperate. They had no warm clothes or goggles and no medicines or bandages. Using whatever materials came to hand, they set about making **splints**, bandages, and makeshift **hammocks**. One of the group's leaders, Fito Strauch, created a device for turning snow into drinking water. Driven by hunger, they survived by eating the flesh of the dead passengers—a decision only taken after much soul-searching. It shocked many people when their story became known.

Inside the wrecked plane, conditions were appalling. Several survivors had broken limbs. Others suffered from frostbite and mountain sickness. At night, it was impossible to move without disturbing the broken arms and legs of the injured.

"Hey, boys," Nicolich shouted, "There's some good news! We just heard it on the radio. They've called off the search."
Inside the crowded cabin, there was silence. As the hopelessness of their predicament enveloped them, they wept.
"Why the hell is that good news?" Páez shouted angrily at Nicolich.
"Because it means," he said, "that we're going to get out of here on our own."

From Piers Paul Read, *Alive!* (1974)

Avalanche!

On the night of October 29, a huge avalanche swept down from the mountain, engulfing the plane and killing eight survivors. After this, the group sprang into action. Three of the strongest members were chosen as "expeditionaries" to go in search of help. On one trip, they found the tail section of the plane, which contained food, clothing, and cigarettes. They also found batteries, which they hoped would allow them to activate the plane's radio. But all attempts to communicate with the outside world failed. Everyone now knew that their only hope was for the three expeditionaries to make a last-ditch trek across the mountains to Chile.

The "Expeditionaries"

Following the avalanche, the hopes of the group rested entirely on the "expeditionaries." These were the three strongest survivors who had been chosen to make the dangerous trek through the mountains in search of help.

To help prepare them for their mission, Fernando Parrado, Antonio "Tintin" Vizintin, and Roberto Canessa were allowed special privileges, including extra rations of food and drink. Daily prayers were said for their health and well-being.

*The survivors huddle in the snow outside the wrecked **fuselage** of the aircraft. On the right, Carlos "Carlitos" Páez can be seen sewing an improvised sleeping bag. Fernando Parrado later wrote: "We needed a way to survive the long nights without freezing, and the quilted insulation we'd taken from the tail section gave us our solution . . ."*

Rescue at Last

On December 12, armed with a sleeping bag made from padding found in the tail section of the plane, Parrado, Canessa, and Vizintin set off on their expedition. Three days later, desperately short of food, Vizintin was forced to turn back. But Parrado and Canessa walked on for another nine days before reaching the banks of a river. As they settled down to rest, they noticed three riders on the opposite bank. Falling to their knees, they shouted across to them, desperately trying to make themselves understood.

The next day, the riders returned with a rescue team. Soon helicopters arrived at the crash site to **airlift** the survivors to safety. After 72 grueling days, the long ordeal of the 16 Andes survivors was over.

Courage and Survival

On their return to Uruguay, the extraordinary story of the survivors was greeted with incredulity. Some were shocked by it. Many more were moved by the courage and resourcefulness of the students. Later the rescuers returned to the crash site and buried the bodies of the dead under a pile of stones. The grave was marked by an iron cross erected in the center of the stone pile.

Beside the wrecked fuselage of the Fairchild, the jubilant survivors greet the arrival of the rescue helicopter—and the end of their long ordeal.

How Would YOU Survive?

After the students returned to Uruguay, many people were shocked to learn that they had survived by eating the flesh of their dead companions. Some even said that the students should have chosen to die instead.

But the Archbishop of Montevideo defended the students: "Morally I see no objection, since it was a question of survival. It is always necessary to eat whatever is at hand, in spite of the repugnance it may evoke."

What do you think? Make a case for and against the students' actions.

ASSAULT ON ANNAPURNA 1

Arlene Blum and the First All-Woman Expedition to the Himalayas

On a golden February morning in 1965, a young American woman hauled herself up an icy slope to stand triumphantly on the summit of Mount Hood, the tallest peak in Oregon. Arlene Blum had trudged all night to reach the top of her very first mountain. At 11,237 feet (3,425 m) above sea level, it was the closest to heaven that she had ever been.

At a time when mountaineering was considered an exclusively male sport, Blum was determined to make a name for herself as a pioneer of women's mountaineering. She spent her youth in pursuit of thrilling adventures across the globe. Most famously, she led an all-woman team to the summit of Annapurna 1 in the Himalayas, the tenth-highest peak in the world—and one of the most dangerous.

All-Woman Team

It was during the late 1970s that Blum first had the idea of organizing an all-woman team to ascend Annapurna 1. Although 90 climbers had attempted the climb, only 8 had reached the summit and all were men. The prospect of becoming one of the first women to attempt such a difficult climb appealed to Blum's sense of adventure. Soon she began to assemble her team.

Born in Chicago in 1945, Arlene Blum came from an Orthodox Jewish family. After a sheltered childhood, she devoted her life to climbing and adventure and has written many books about the challenge of mountaineering.

Choosing the Team

Blum knew that only the best climbers could attempt a climb as dangerous as Annapurna 1. She and two of her fellow climbers decided to select the applicants by taking them on a training climb into the Sierra Nevada in Spain. After a few days, Blum had selected a team of 12 tough and strong-willed women.

The next challenge was raising funds for the expedition. Blum had a hard time convincing people to invest money in an all-woman climbing team. But with the help of some eye-catching tee-shirts, the team finally raised the money they needed, and the expedition set off for Kathmandu.

Above: Arlene Blum (front row, right) and members of the 1978 American Women's Himalayan Expedition

Below: The Annapurna is not one mountain, but a 177 foot (54 km) string of connected peaks, of which Annapurna 1 (26,545 feet, or 8,091 m) is the highest. The constant risk of avalanches makes it one of the most dangerous mountain ranges in the world.

Annapurna 1

Towering over the surrounding region, Annapurna 1 is located east of a great gorge cut through the Himalayas by the Kali Gandaki River. Annapurna is a Sanskrit name meaning "Goddess of the Harvests." In the Hindu religion, Annapurna is a goddess of **fertility** and agriculture.

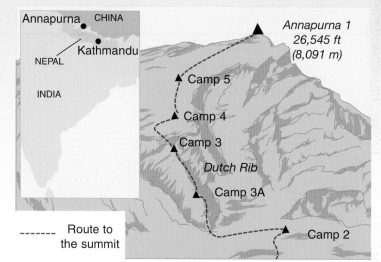

Annapurna   CHINA

Kathmandu

NEPAL

INDIA

Annapurna 1
26,545 ft
(8,091 m)

Camp 5

Camp 4

Camp 3

Dutch Rib

Camp 3A

Camp 2

- - - - - - - Route to the summit

In Sight of Annapurna

On arrival in Nepal, the climbers, Sherpa guides, kitchen staff, and porters trekked for 12 days through **monsoon** rains before reaching North Base Camp. The vast summit of Annapurna 1 loomed 2 miles (3.2 km) vertically above.

After establishing Camp 1 at 16,400 feet (5,000 m) and planning another five camps along their route, the team needed to decide who was going to lead on the steep slopes. Without consulting the others, Blum chose the four best ice climbers. To her dismay, the other women were not at all happy with her plan—and even more angry at not being consulted. After much discussion, it was eventually decided to stick with her plan. Peace was restored. After a brief ceremony to ask the mountain spirits for a safe and successful ascent, the group set out to tackle the highest slopes.

"I'd never done anything physical my whole life. My first few climbs, I was catastrophically bad and uniquely incompetent. But the first time I got on a glacier, I had this instant recognition that this was the most beautiful, peaceful, happy place I'd ever been."

From Arlene Blum,
Breaking Trail: A Climber's Life (2006)

In Sight of the Summit

After storms and avalanches, the morning of September 25 dawned brilliantly clear as Blum and two other climbers carried the first loads up to Camp 3A, a temporary staging area for the difficult climb along the narrow ridge **crest** to the permanent Camp 3. Their spirits soared as they made it to the crest of the Dutch Rib. The group's next challenge was breaking a trail along the knife-edged crest of the rib itself, which snaked up like the twisting tail of a dragon for over .6 miles (1 km).

Finally at 3:30 P.M. on October 15, 1978, four climbers reached the top and proudly unfurled an American flag, a Nepalese flag, and an expedition flag, all held together by a "Save the Whales" pin. They had become the first women and the first Americans to climb Annapurna 1.

*Climbing the twisting crest of the Dutch Rib, the climbers faced soft, unstable snow and huge **cornices**. "It was grueling and scary work," Blum wrote later.*

Missing

There was jubilation as the news of the ascent reached the camps below. But when a second summit team failed to make contact by radio as planned, the mood gradually turned to concern. By evening, the two climbers were still missing, and the rest of the women's team were feeling more and more anxious.

Mountain Memorial

The next morning, Blum woke early and continued calling for the missing pair. The others scoured the slope around Camp 5 with binoculars and called over and over. No response.

A couple of days later, the Sherpas returned from the mountain with the news the women had been dreading: they had found the bodies of Vera Watson and Alison Chadwick-Onyszkiewicz.

The loss of two members was a devastating blow to the team. Slowly, they packed up their heavy loads and made their way down to base camp. But before they left, Blum chipped out the two women's names on a memorial stone. They would be engraved forever in the rock, facing the summit they had so hoped to reach.

"As the others headed for the top, I went down to Camp II by myself, and found myself thinking: 'What's a nice Jewish girl from the Midwest doing teetering backwards on a narrow ridge at 21,000 feet?'"

From Arlene Blum,
Breaking Trail: A Climber's Life (2006)

What Makes a Team Leader?

One of Arlene Blum's reasons for organizing the All-Woman Himalayan Expedition was to prove to the world that women could achieve success in a tough "man's sport."

Take another look at her story:

1 What qualities do you think Blum showed as a team leader?

2 What things do you think would have been handled differently if the team had been all male?

3 Why do you think Blum's childhood might have made her want to set out on a life of adventure?

TO HELL AND BACK

The Incredible Story of Joe Simpson and Simon Yates

In June 1985, two young British climbers set out to conquer the unclimbed west face of the remote 21,000 feet (6,400 m) high Siula Grande in the Peruvian Andes. Neither Joe Simpson nor Simon Yates had climbed higher than 18,000 feet (5,500 m) before, but they had every reason to feel optimistic. Both were skilled and experienced mountaineers. What could possibly go wrong?

The first two days of the climb brought their fair share of narrow escapes. On day one, a minor avalanche almost swept Yates off the mountain. Blizzards and frequent rock falls added to their problems. At one point, Simpson found himself "gripped"—a climber's term for being paralyzed by panic—on a horribly exposed section of rock with 3,937 feet (1,200 m) of thin air below him. But it was not until the two had reached the summit and had begun to make their descent that a truly spectacular chain of disasters began to unfold.

ATLANTIC
OCEAN

Siula Grande
21,000 ft
(6,400 m)

PERU

SOUTH
AMERICA

Lima

PACIFIC
OCEAN

Below: The soaring peak of the Siula Grande in the Peruvian Andes

Ice Wall

Simpson had just swung over the top of a 26 foot (8 m) **ice wall** on the northern ridge and was searching for a hold, when there was a sharp crack. Before he knew it, he was falling.

Yates hurried to the scene to find his friend lying in agony at the foot of the ice wall. His first thought was that Simpson was as good as dead. The last two days had brought them close to exhaustion. Food and water were running low. It would be hard enough for Yates to reach safety on his own, without carrying Simpson down with him.

Hanging in Space

No mountaineer would have blamed Yates for leaving Simpson where he lay. But instead, he and Simpson came up with a plan. Knotting two ropes together, Yates would lower the injured Simpson as far as the rope would allow, then climb down after him, and so on, down the slope.

Amazingly, it seemed to work—until suddenly Simpson found himself sliding faster than usual. It could only mean one thing: he was heading for the edge of a sheer drop. Screaming frantically, he tried to stop himself, but the snow was too loose and powdery to get a grip. Helplessly, he careered off the edge of the mountain and found himself dangling in space above a huge crevasse.

Simpson searches for a foothold on the wall of sheer ice, in a scene from the film based on Joe Simpson's bestselling book Touching the Void.

Dragged to Disaster

Far above him, and unable to see what had happened, Yates, too, was powerless. He could feel by the weight on the rope that Simpson was hanging in space—but he was in danger himself. The shallow seat which he had dug in the snow was collapsing. Inch by inch, Simpson's weight was dragging Yates toward the precipice.

Forced to choose between saving himself or risking both their deaths, Yates made the most agonizing decision any climber can face. He cut the rope.

Beyond Help

Tortured by guilt, Yates spent the night on the mountain. The following morning he found a way down the rest of the slope. Seeing the crevasse, he guessed what must have happened. He shouted down it. No answer came. Convinced that Simpson could never have survived the fall, he turned and headed towards base camp.

Clinging to the rope with frostbitten fingers and grimacing with pain from his broken leg, Joe Simpson is swept off the mountain to find himself dangling in space over a 100 foot (30 m) drop.

"Half an hour passed. I stopped shouting at Simon. I knew he was in the same situation as me, unable to move. Either he would die in his seat or be pulled from it by the constant strain of my body. I wondered whether I would die before this happened . . ."

From Joe Simpson, *Touching the Void* (1988)

Tomb of Ice

But unknown to Yates, Simpson had survived. Lying on an ice bridge deep within the crevasse, he pulled on the rope. To his surprise, it went slack. Hauling it in, he found the frayed end. It had clearly been cut.

Now it was Simpson's turn to face an agonizing choice. Climbing up the sides of the crevasse was out of the question. But should he crawl even deeper down in the hope of finding a side exit or stay on the ice bridge and die? There could only be one answer. Grimacing with pain, he began his descent.

Back from the Dead

Three days after leaving his companion for dead on the Siula Grande, Simon Yates awoke in the small hours of the morning to hear faint sounds from the darkness outside his tent. Straining his ears, he heard a tortured voice calling: "S-I-I-M-O-O-N!" It was Simpson.

Incredibly, Simpson had inched his way out of the crevasse and dragged his body an unimaginable 6 miles (10 km) across snow, ice, and jagged boulders back to base camp. After two nights in the open, he was exhausted, **dehydrated,** and **delirious**—but alive!

How Would YOU Survive?

Joe Simpson's struggle for survival is one of the great adventure stories of modern times.

When Simpson's book, *Touching the Void,* was first published, some climbers criticized Simon Yates for cutting the rope to avoid being dragged over the edge of the precipice. Simpson always defended his friend's action.

What do you think? What would you have done?

In a scene from the film Touching the Void, *a dazed, dehydrated, and exhausted Joe Simpson begins his agonizing journey down the mountain.*

Glossary

air traffic control ground-based airport staff who use radar to track aircraft in flight and give instructions to pilots who are taking off and landing

airlift to rescue trapped people by helicopter or plane

avalanche a mass of snow and ice that crashes down a mountain slope, gathering speed and size as it descends; avalanches are a constant danger to climbers on high mountain slopes

base camp the starting point for a mountaineering expedition, where supplies of food and equipment are stored

blizzard a severe winter storm with freezing cold winds and heavy blowing snow

cascade a waterfall or series of waterfalls

cornice an overhanging mass of ice or snow on the ridge of a mountain

crest the top of a hill or a wave

crevasse a deep, open crack in a mass of snow or ice

dehydrated suffering from lack of water; symptoms of dehydration include dizziness, decreased blood pressure, and fainting

delirious mentally confused or disturbed, usually as a result of fever or extreme physical stress

fertility the ability to grow crops or fruit or to reproduce or bear young; gods or goddesses of fertility are worshipped in some countries in order to ensure a good harvest

fuselage the part of a plane occupied by crew, passengers, and cargo

hammock a hanging bed made from strong material and attached by hooks at either end to supports

ice wall a steep or near-vertical mass of ice

metal pegs pegs hammered into cracks in the rock, to which climbing ropes can be attached

monsoon the rainy season in India and Southeast Asia

ridge a long, narrow part of a hill or mountain

rock fall a shower of falling stones and rock, usually caused by erosion of a cliff face or mountainside

satellite navigation determining where you are using information from satellites orbiting Earth

Sherpa an inhabitant of the mountainous region of Nepal; Sherpa mountain guides and climbers are renowned for their hardiness, skill, and experience at high altitude

splint a straight piece of wood or metal used to support and protect a broken arm, leg, or other bone

summit the highest point of a mountain, measured in feet or meters above sea level

Victorian Age the period in British history from 1837 to 1901, coinciding with the reign of Queen Victoria

Index

Alps 4-7
Andes 5, 16, 20, 26
Annapurna 21-24
avalanche 4, 5, 7, 9, 19, 22, 24, 26

base camp 13, 23, 25, 28, 29
blizzard 5, 11, 26
Blum, Arlene 21-25

crevasse 12, 13, 27, 28, 29
Curicó 16

Dutch Rib 22, 24

Everest 4, 5, 11-15

Hillary, Edmund 11-15
Himalayas 5, 11, 12, 15, 21, 22, 25

Irvine, Andrew 4, 11

Khumbu Icefall 12, 13

Mallory, George 4, 5, 11
Matterhorn 6-10
Messner, Reinhold 5, 11
Mount Hood 21

Sherpa 4, 12, 13, 15, 23, 25

Sierra Nevada 22
Simpson, Joe 26-29
Siula Grande 26, 29
Stella Maris College 16
summit 4-9, 11, 12, 13-15, 21, 22, 23-26

Tenzing, Norgay 11-15

Whymper, Edward 6-10

Yates, Simon 26-29

Web Finder

Classic photographs from the early days of mountaineering
http://www.alpine-club.org.uk/photolibrary/album.html

Photographs of Everest expeditions from the archives
of the Royal Geographical Society and The Institute of
British Geographers
http://imagingeverest.rgs.org

Dramatic slide-show of Arlene Blum's 1978 American
Women's Himalayan Expedition
http://www.arleneblum.com/photo_album.html

Joe Simpson's official Web site includes remarkable
photographs of his return to the Siula Grande for the
filming of *Touching the Void*
http://www.noordinaryjoe.co.uk/gallery.asp